Magic, Myth, and Mystery

WEREWO

DO YOU BELIEVE?

This series features creatures that excite our minds. They're magical. They're mythical. They're mysterious. They're also not real. They live in our stories. They're brought to life by our imaginations. Facts about these creatures are based on folklore, legends, and beliefs. We have a rich history of believing in the impossible. But these creatures only live in fantasies and dreams. Monsters do not live under our beds. They live in our heads!

45th Parallel Press

Published in the United States of America by Cherry Lake Publishing
Ann Arbor, Michigan
www.cherrylakepublishing.com

Reading Adviser: Marla Conn MS, Ed., Literacy specialist, Read-Ability, Inc.
Book Design: Felicia Macheske

Photo Credits: © S-BELOV/Shutterstock.com, cover; © Stockimo/Shutterstock.com, 1; © welburnstuart/Shutterstock.com, 5; © Marcin Perkowski/Shutterstock.com, 7; © Semmick Photo/Shutterstock.com, 8; © Gleb Semenjuk/Shutterstock.com, 11; © Valentina Photos/Shutterstock.com, 13; © Martin Mecnarowski/Shutterstock.com, 15; © Vuk Kostic/Shutterstock.com, 16; © Pepgooner/Shutterstock.com, 19; © Kiselev Andrey Valerevich/Shutterstock.com, 20; © Fernando Cortes/Shutterstock.com, 22; © Todd Keith/iStock, 25; © Vuk Kostic/Shutterstock.com, 27; © welcomia/Shutterstock.com, 28;

Graphic Elements Throughout: © denniro/Shutterstock.com; © Libellule/Shutterstock.com; © sociologas/Shutterstock.com; © paprika/Shutterstock.com; © ilolab/Shutterstock.com; © Bruce Rolff/Shutterstock.com

45th Parallel Press is an imprint of Cherry Lake Publishing.

Library of Congress Cataloging-in-Publication Data

Names: Loh-Hagan, Virginia, author.
Title: Werewolves : magic, myth, and mystery / by Virginia Loh-Hagan.
Description: Ann Arbor : Cherry Lake Publishing, [2016] | Series: Magic, myth, and mystery | Includes bibliographical references and index.
Identifiers: LCCN 2016004926| ISBN 9781634711104 (hardcover) | ISBN 9781634713085 (pbk.) | ISBN 9781634712095 (pdf) | ISBN 9781634714075 (ebook)
Subjects: LCSH: Werewolves—Juvenile literature. | Animals, Mythical—Juvenile literature.
Classification: LCC GR830.W4 L64 2016 | DDC 398.24/54—dc23
LC record available at http://lccn.loc.gov/2016004926

Cherry Lake Publishing would like to acknowledge the work of The Partnership for 21st Century Skills. Please visit *www.p21.org* for more information.

Printed in the United States of America
Corporate Graphics Inc.

TABLE of CONTENTS

Chapter One

Hairy and Howling

What are werewolves?
What do werewolves look like?

"Owoooo!" Werewolves are scary!

Werewolves are humans. These humans **shift**. Shift means to change. They change into wolves. They have to shift during full moons. Full moons have power. Werewolves are drawn to them. They're strongest during full moons.

Werewolves hunt. They kill. They feast. They **crave flesh**. Crave means to want. Flesh is meat. They eat live humans. They eat newly dead bodies. They tear limbs. They rip flesh. They crack bones.

New werewolves can't control themselves under a full moon.
Older werewolves have more control.

Explained by Science!

Some people are hairy. This doesn't mean they're werewolves. They might have hypertrichosis. This condition is sometimes called werewolf syndrome. It's rare. There are fewer than 100 reported cases. It sometimes runs in families. Hypertrichosis makes people grow thick hair. Some grow hair all over. Some grow hair in certain places. Men grow hair covering their faces and eyelids. Women grow thick patches on their bodies. Some people have extreme cases. They have naevoid hypertrichosis. They grow a lot of hair all over their bodies. They have hair that sticks up. They have tails. They have one hairy eyebrow. They have hairy beards. They really look like werewolves.

There are different types of shapeshifters. Some witches can turn into ravens.

Werewolves are **shapeshifters**. They change their shapes. They change their forms.

Shapeshifters shift for different reasons. They shift when sensing danger. They shift when dreaming. They shift when mad.

A wolfman isn't a werewolf. They're different. A wolfman is a wolf and a man. He's both at the same time. He's both all the time. He has a human body. He's covered in wolf hair. He has claws. He has fangs.

Werewolves have human forms. They look like regular humans. But some may look different. They have curved fingernails. They walk with a swing. They have long eyebrows. Their tongues have **bristles**. Bristles are short, stiff hairs. They have big hands. They have long middle fingers.

Werewolves have wolf forms. They look like huge wolves. They're hairy. They don't have tails. They have human eyes. Some may have yellow eyes. They have pointy ears. They have sharp claws. They have fangs. They have sharp teeth. They can speak.

If werewolves are cut when in human form, their wounds have fur in them.

Chapter Two

Beware of the Wolf Pack

What are the powers of werewolves? What's the power of a werewolf pack?

Werewolves are beasts. They're powerful. They're stronger than humans. They're stronger than wolves. They have super strength. They're fast. They're flexible. They move gracefully. They climb walls. They dent steel. They rip doors. They don't feel pain. They have **stamina**. This means they don't get tired.

They have super senses. They see well. They have **night vision**. They can see in total darkness. They hear well. They smell well. They smell 100 times better than humans can.

It is said that werewolves are stronger than polar bears.

When Fantasy Meets Reality!

Lykoi cats are called werewolf cats. They're named after the Greek word for wolf. They look like werewolves. They're a mix of two cats. The cats are sphynx cat and black domestic shorthair cat. There was a mutation. A mutation is a change in genes. The change stopped hair growth. The Lykoi cats have a special hair pattern. They look scraggly and patchy. They have thin hair. They don't have fur around their nose, eyes, underbelly, or paws. They shed. At times, they can be almost bald. They have strong immune systems. They act like dogs. They wag their tails. Johnny Gobble is an animal doctor. He's breeding them. He said that the first kittens "looked like little hunting dogs running around on the carpet. I thought it was neat." The cats usually cost $1,500 to $2,500.

Werewolves sense each other's pain and death.

Werewolves work as a **pack**. A pack is a wolf family. They talk. They howl. They listen for echoes. They talk through **telepathy**. They read minds. They talk without saying words out loud. This makes them better hunters. They trap prey. They circle prey. They attack as a pack.

They have super healing powers. They heal fast. They restore their bodies. They regrow body parts. They're **immune** to human sicknesses. This means they're not affected.

They don't live forever. But they age slowly. They're healthy for a long time.

Chapter Three

Slaying the Beasts

**What are werewolves' weaknesses?
How can werewolves be killed?**

Werewolves have weaknesses. They hate silver. Silver is pure. It's connected to the moon. It won't kill werewolves. But it'll hurt them. It'll weaken them. It burns their insides. **Quicksilver** will kill them. It's liquid mercury. It's poisonous.

Werewolves hate **wolfsbane**. Wolfsbane is a plant. It has deadly poison. Werewolves hate salt. Salt sucks water from their bodies. These things keep werewolves away. They stop werewolves. But they won't kill them.

Werewolves also hate the same things as wolves.

Many believe silver bullets will kill werewolves.

Werewolves have weak moments. They're weak when returning to human form. They're tired. They're confused. They're weak before shifting. Electricity stops the change.

Werewolves hate vampires. They fight them. Many have died fighting vampires.

Werewolves are hard to kill. But they can be killed. Their heads can be chopped off. Their hearts can be cut out. Their brains can be crushed.

SURVIVAL TIPS!

- Cover up human smell. Rub mud on clothes. Rub mud on skin.

- Position yourself upwind. This is so human smells don't reach the werewolf.

- Stay in crowds, especially at night. Werewolves stay away from crowds.

- Don't play dead. Werewolves can smell you.

- Get inside and/or stay inside. Hide. Stay out of sight.

- Don't yell insults. Don't curse. Don't be aggressive. This'll make werewolves mad. Werewolves are half-human. They understand your words.

- Aim for the eyes. Werewolves have a wider skull than humans. Their eyes and forehead are good targets.

Chapter Four

Beastly Changes

**How do people become werewolves?
How do werewolves change?**

There are different ways to become a werewolf. Some humans aren't given a choice.

Werewolves feed on humans. They bite. But some humans survive. They get **infected**. Infect means to spread a sickness. Deep werewolf scratches also infect. These humans become werewolves. It happens against their will.

Some are born as werewolves. They have two

werewolf parents. They don't have a choice. They're born into a pack. It's their way of life.

Different cultures have different beliefs about werewolves.

Some werewolves choose. They want to be werewolves.

Some use magic. They remove their clothes. They wear a magical belt. The belt is wolf's skin. Some wear the whole wolf skin. Some use magic creams. They rub creams into their skin. Some drink magic **potions**. Potions are mixes.

Some find wolf paw prints. They wait for rain. They drink water from the print. Some eat raw wolf brains.

Some wait for a full moon. They do a devil dance. They sleep outside. They put their face to the moon. The moon shines on them.

Some humans made pacts with the devil to become a werewolf.

Humans get sick after turning. They get fevers. They get chills. They're thirsty. They itch. They suffer for two days. Then they grow into their werewolf bodies.

Shifting is a process. The process is quick. It takes several minutes. But it's painful. Bones grow longer. They change shape. They move. They burst through skin. Skin changes. Organs move around. Muscles move around. Fur sprouts out. Skulls change shape.

Dying werewolves shift. They return to human form. They die as humans.

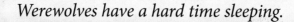

Werewolves have a hard time sleeping.

Know the Lingo!

- **Alpha:** leader of the pack

- **Bane:** evil spirits

- **Biter:** werewolf who tries to change as many humans as possible

- **City-wolf:** werewolf who lives in the city

- **Cub-born:** werewolf born in wolf form

- **Deader:** werewolf slang word for vampire

- **Dogpile:** a brutal attack or fight

- **Feral:** werewolf who has forgotten its human identity

- **Garou:** French word for werewolf

- **Harrying:** harassing or chasing prey until they get tired

- **Lupine:** sharing characteristics with a wolf

- **Lycanthrope:** another word for werewolf

- **Skinwalkers:** Native American word for shapeshifters

- **Tooth-and-claw:** fighting like wolves, not humans

- **Turnskin:** someone who can change skin at will

- **Were:** man who changes shape

Chapter Five

Werewolf Curse

What is the werewolf curse?
What are some werewolf stories?

Werewolves may be **cursed**. Curses are punishments. Something happened a long time ago. A human did something bad. A force cursed the human. (The force could be a god. It could be a witch.) The force made the human a werewolf. That werewolf infected others.

There's a Greek story about this. Zeus is a god. He visited King Lycaon. The king didn't believe it was Zeus. He fed Zeus human flesh. Zeus got mad.

He punished the king. He turned the king into a wolf. Lycaon may be the first werewolf.

Curses are hard to break.

Real-World Connection

The Quileute are Native Americans. They live in Washington State. They were featured in the Twilight stories. They were featured as werewolves. There's some truth to this. The tribe is connected to wolves. Wolves live in their area. Their folklore indicates their tribe started as two wolves. Q'waeti was a powerful changer. He saw the wolves. He changed them into humans. The humans became the Quileute tribe. Quileute warriors belong to the Wolf Society. They protect the tribe. They wear headdresses shaped like wolves' heads. They have ceremonies. They do wolf dances. They get power from wolves. The Quileute feature wolves in their songs, stories, and art.

It is said that a werewolf attacked southern France. It's the "Beast of Gévaudan." This happened in the 1700s. It looked like a wolf.

The beast ripped out throats. It ate body parts. It killed over 100 people. It injured 40 people.

Hunters tried to kill it. They shot it. But the beast was unharmed. People believed it was a werewolf. Finally, the army killed it. They found human parts in the beast's stomach. Werewolf stories spread.

Werewolf stories changed over time.

The Beast of Bray Road is Wisconsin's werewolf. It looks like a wolfman. It's hairy. It's the size of a bear. It's 7 feet (2 meters) tall. It's 4 feet (1.2 m) when on all fours. It walks on its hind legs. It weighs 700 pounds (317.5 kilograms). Its fur is brown and gray. It has pointy ears. It has fangs. It has yellow eyes. It has human fingers.

No one has seen it shift. But some people think it's a werewolf. The Beast of Bray Road is famous. It's a modern American werewolf story.

European immigrants brought werewolf stories to the United States.

Did You Know?

A werewoman is a female shapeshifter. She doesn't have to be a wolf. She can be any animal. She uses the same change process as a werewolf.

Some people think werewolf legends explain serial killers. A serial killer is someone who kills many people. Werewolves were blamed for murders.

Some werewolves remove their clothes before changing. Some people believe their clothes turn to stone. Werewolves return to their human forms. Then the stones become clothes again.

Some people linked werewolves to puberty. Puberty is when children change to adults. People thought teenagers were more likely to become werewolves during puberty. They grow body hair. They're moody. They grow stronger.

There were good werewolves. Latvian and Lithuanian legends featured good werewolves. These werewolves brought humans treasure.

Some Eastern European legends feature dead werewolves becoming vampires. The Slavic word for werewolf is *volkodlak*. It means "vampire" in the Serbian language.

Scandinavian Vikings have werewolf stories. Ulfhednars were warriors. They dressed up in wolf skins. They took over the wolves' spirits. They fought like wolves in battle. They didn't feel pain. They killed their enemies in a frenzy.

In the United States, there's insurance for werewolf damage. People have also insured themselves against becoming werewolves.

Consider This!

Take a Position: Werewolves are known to be half-man and half-wolf. But some believe werewolves aren't humans at all. Do you think werewolves can claim to be human? Argue your point with reasons and evidence.

Say What? Read 45th Parallel Press's book about vampires. Explain vampires' strengths and weaknesses. Reread this book about werewolves. Explain werewolves' strengths and weaknesses. Which monster would win in a battle? Explain your reasoning.

Think About It! Some sources claim that silver kills werewolves. Other sources claim that silver only hurts werewolves. Why do you think there are such differences?

Learn More

- Bingham, Jane. *Vampires and Werewolves*. Chicago: Heinemann-Raintree, 2014.

- McCollum, Sean. *Werewolves: The Truth Behind History's Scariest Shape-Shifters*. Mankato, MN: Capstone Press, 2016.

- Valentino, Serena. *How to Be a Werewolf: The Claws-On Guide for the Modern Lycanthrope*. Somerville, MA: Candlewick, 2011.

Glossary

bristles (BRIS-uhlz) short, stiff hairs

crave (KRAVE) to want

cursed (KURSD) punished

flesh (FLESH) meat muscle

immune (ih-MYOON) to not be affected by

infected (in-FEKT-id) to get a sickness

night vision (NITE VIZH-uhn) the ability to see in darkness

pack (PAK) wolf family

potions (POH-shuhnz) mixtures

quicksilver (KWIK-sil-vur) liquid mercury

shapeshifters (SHAYP-shift-urz) monsters that change forms

shift (SHIFT) to change

stamina (STAM-uh-nuh) the ability to not get tired

telepathy (tuh-LEP-uh-thee) the ability to read minds and speak without saying words

wolfsbane (WULFS-bayn) a poisonous plant

Index

About the Author

Dr. Virginia Loh-Hagan is an author, university professor, former classroom teacher, and curriculum designer. Her dogs howl at full moons, fireworks, postal workers, gardeners ... the list goes on. She lives in San Diego with her very tall husband and very naughty dogs. To learn more about her, visit www.virginialoh.com.